# Shoes!

## A Footwear Fashion Frolic

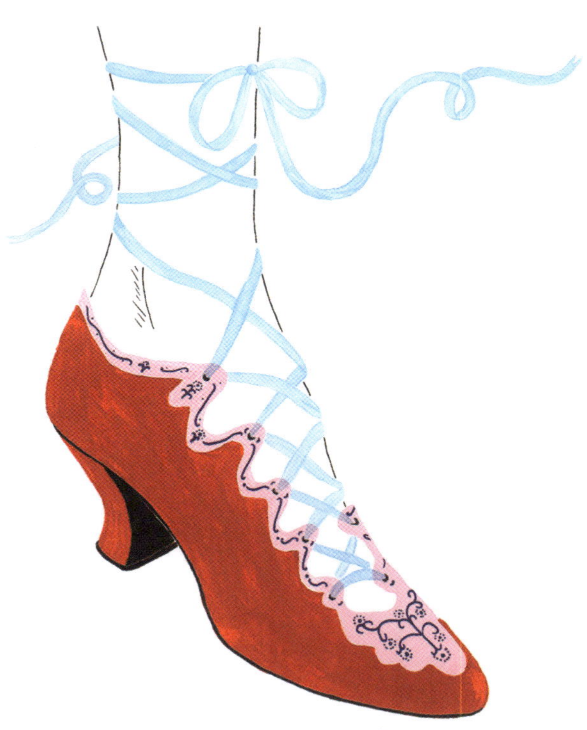

Anna Davies & Daisy Wynter

# Contents:

Chapter 1

# SHOES

## (AND WHY WE LOVE THEM!)

# SHOES!

## (AND WHY WE LOVE THEM)

"Craziness in a shoe is great! You can exaggerate and it doesn't feel stupid. But to have too much craziness near your face, that would just feel weird."

Miuccia Prada

Over the past 30 years, the average number of shoes owned by women has doubled. Sneakers, heels, flats, boots - we just can't seem to get enough! But what is it about shoes that makes them so irresistible?

As humans, we have large brains but soft feet. Without hooves or tough footpads for protection, we created shoes to shield and support our delicate tootsies. However, over time, shoes have become much more than a mere practicality. From towering stilettos to bold platform sneakers, footwear is a way to express personality, wealth, cultural background and status. Throughout history, the stories shoes tell have evolved — and so have the styles.

Leather naturally breaks down over time, which means there's limited evidence about the earliest footwear humans used. However, ancient skeletons suggest that people began wearing shoes around 40,000 years ago – likely simple coverings made from animal hides wrapped around the feet.

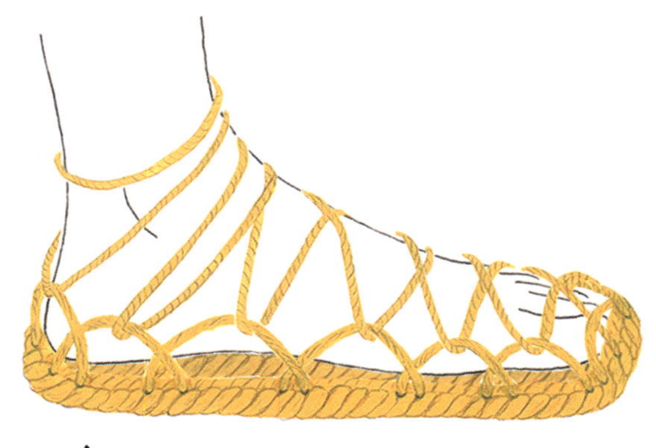

## Ancestral Puebloans

These braided yucca fibre sandals date from around 10,000 years ago. They were worn by the Ancestral Puebloan people of the American Southwest.

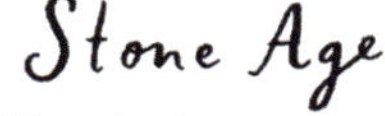

## Stone Age

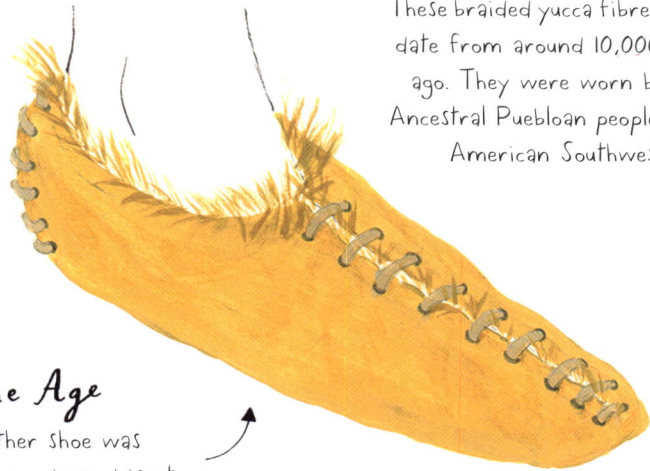

This leather shoe was found in Armenia and is at least 5,500 years old.

## Paduka

Wooden paduka sandals have been worn in India for thousands of years. They are held on with a knob between the big and first toe. The Hindu god, Krishna, is often depicted wearing padukas.

# EARLY SHOES

Ancient Romans were obsessed with status. People from different social classes wore different types of shoes.

Calceus
Short, decorative, laced boots worn by noblemen.
Pattern for a Carbatina
Carbatina
Poor people wore these very simple shoes made of a single piece of leather. They had no proper sole.
Caligae
Heavy, hobnailed sandals worn by soldiers. When they marched in unison the sandals made a formidable sound.

As history unfolded, there were some unusual moments in shoe design...

## Kabkabs

Kabkabs were wooden stilt-shoes that were popular in the Middle East in the 14th century as a way of keeping the wearer's feet away from the muddy streets. As the years went on, they grew taller and taller. By the 1600s, they were reaching heights of almost half a metre!

## Poulaines

Poulaines were worn by men and women in the Middle Ages. They had pointed toes that stretched well beyond the wearer's feet. Some tied the toes to their knees so they wouldn't trip over.

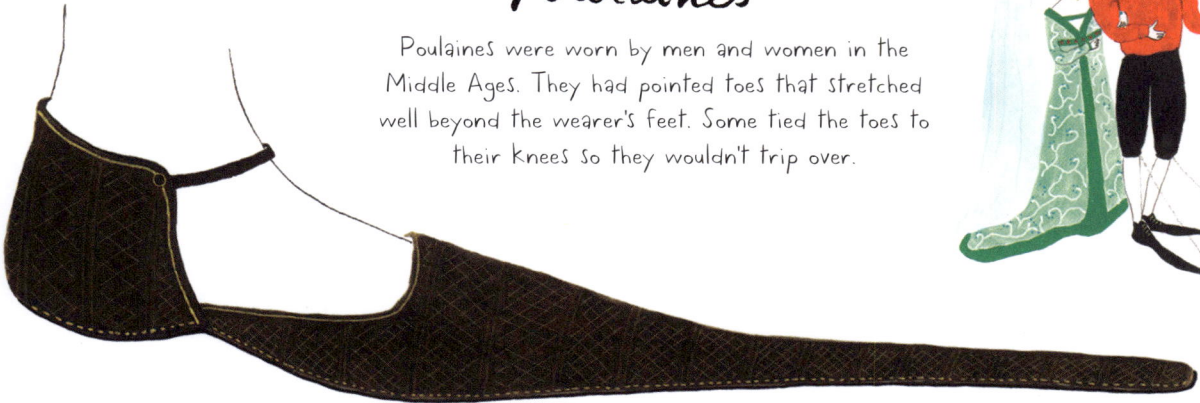

## Louis XIV

In the court of Louis XIV of France, the king and his noblemen wore bejewelled high heels painted red to show off their shapely calves.

# The Victorian Era

"If the feet are small, well-shod, and prettily used in walking, they add an additional charm to the appearance, and are an indication of high standing and of gentle birth."

- Victorian Ladies' Magazine

Owww...

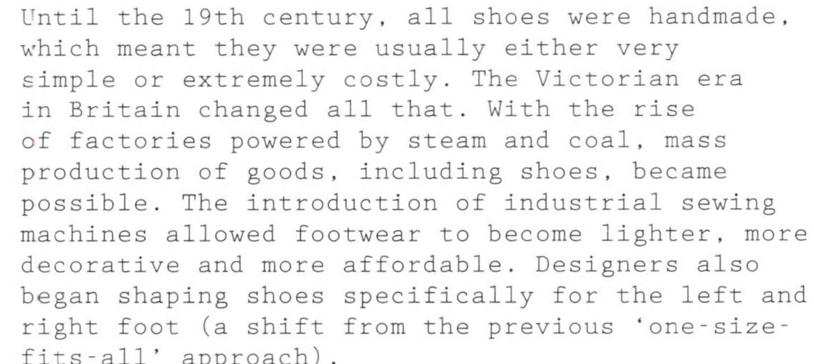

Until the 19th century, all shoes were handmade, which meant they were usually either very simple or extremely costly. The Victorian era in Britain changed all that. With the rise of factories powered by steam and coal, mass production of goods, including shoes, became possible. The introduction of industrial sewing machines allowed footwear to become lighter, more decorative and more affordable. Designers also began shaping shoes specifically for the left and right foot (a shift from the previous 'one-size-fits-all' approach).

The Victorians were very aware of social classes, and fashion was an important way for people to express their status.

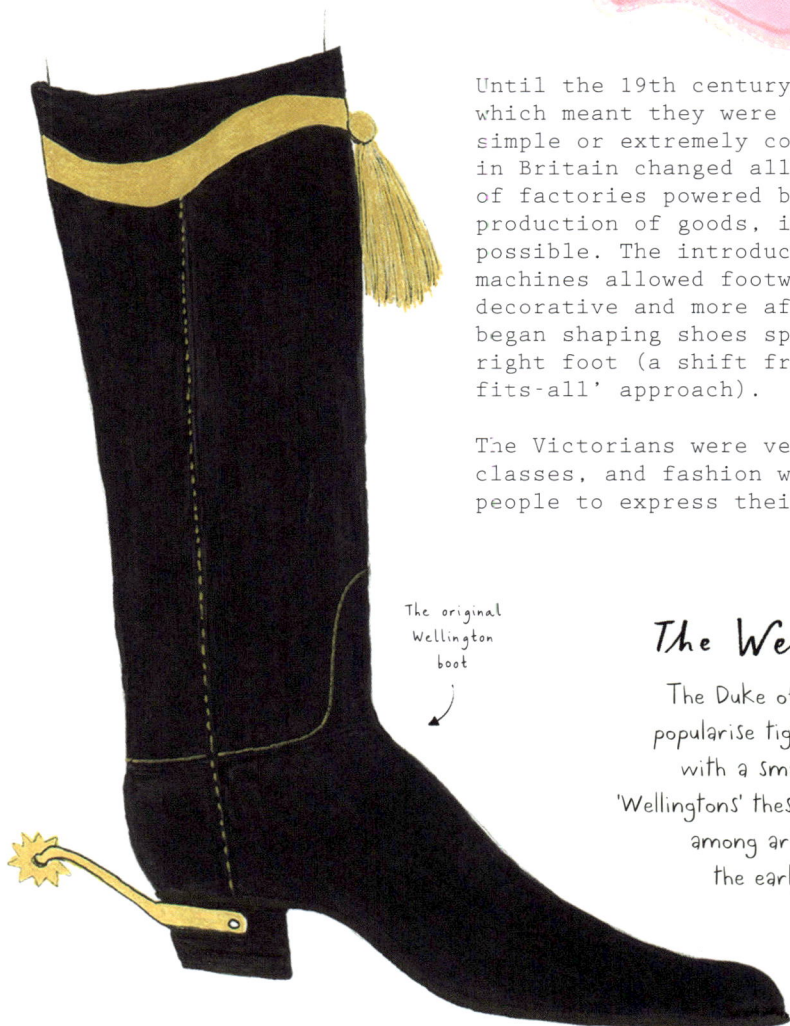

The original Wellington boot

## The Wellington Boot

The Duke of Wellington helped popularise tight, calf-length boots with a small heel. Known as 'Wellingtons' these boots became a staple among aristocratic men in the early 19th century.

## Queen Victoria's Boots

Women also wore leather boots, typically fastened with side buttons. In 1837, British inventor, J. Sparkes Hall, presented Queen Victoria with the first pair of boots featuring an elastic side gusset. This easy-to-wear, slip-on style quickly gained popularity among both men and women.

By the late Victorian period, women mostly wore high-heeled boots with pointed toes. For evening wear, they wore elaborate silk shoes that were so delicate they could only be worn indoors.

Bright silk shoes were designed to match a gown, a sash or ribbons in the hat of the wealthy wearer.

# ANATOMY of a SHOE

Insole
The inside bottom of the shoe, which the foot rests on. In sports shoes, this usually has some cushioning.
Upper
The body of the shoe, which holds the foot.
Tongue
The strip of leather that keeps the laces away from the foot.
Vamp
The section of the upper that covers the foot and reaches backwards to the sole.
Heel
The elevated section under the heel of the foot. It can be high or flat.
Toe Box
The part of the shoe that covers and protects the toes.
Welt
The strip of leather or rubber that connects the upper to the sole.
Sole
The bottom of the shoe.

# What a Heel!

1. Cuban: A chunky, short to medium height heel, which tapers from top to bottom.
2. Slingback: A heeled shoe with a strap that secures the shoe in place.
3. Mule: A slip-on shoe with covered toes and an open back.
4. Wedge: A shoe where one thick piece of material serves as both the sole and the heel. It became very popular in the 1970s.
5. Block: A chunky, square heel for better stability.
6. Spool or Louis: A short heel with an hourglass shape, like a spool of cotton.
7. Flared: A chunky heel that is wider at the bottom than the top.
8. Cone: A heel with a thick top that tapers to a slimmer base.
9. Platform: A high heel with a thick sole under the ball of the foot.
10. Kitten: A short, slim heel.
11. Stiletto: A tall, skinny heel that came into fashion in the 1950s. The name means dagger in Italian.

# IF THE SHOE FITS...

These are some classic formal and casual shoe types that are popular today. They can come in all sorts of materials and their shapes have been interpreted and re-interpreted by shoe designers through the decades.

**Brogue**

A sturdy shoe with decorative holes in the leather upper.

**Loafer**

A slip-on shoe with a strap across the inset.

**Chelsea Boot**

Ankle boots with elastic side panels and a tab at the back to help pull them on.

**Winklepicker**

Shoes and boots with long, sharp pointed toes inspired by medieval footwear and worn by rockers in the 1950s.

**Oxford**

A formal shoe with the eyelets sewn under the vamp (a closed lacing system) to create a sleek appearance.

Deck Shoe
A casual loafer with simple laces. It usually has a white sole so it doesn't mark the boat's deck.
Creeper
A shoe with a thick crepe sole and a suede upper.
Sandal
An open, strappy shoe for warm weather.
Court Shoe
A slip-on shoe with a low-cut front. Also known as a pump.
Chukka Boot
Simple, ankle-high boots with two or three eyelets.
Cowboy Boot
A riding boot made popular in America with a stacked heel and decorative stitching.

Chapter 2

# STEPPING THROUGH TIME

## Shoe Design Across the 20th Century

# The 1900s

During the First World War (1914-1918), men went off to fight and women filled their boots. Literally. They were workers now, and they needed shoes that were more practical than they had been in the past.

The newly popular bicycle gave women greater freedom.

Due to fabric shortages, dresses got shorter, and so, as modesty was still very important, tall boots became very popular. They were made of leather or canvas and were laced or buttoned to mid-calf height. Later in the 1910s, shorter boots became more common.

Hemlines rose from floor-length to mid-calf.

Ladies lace-up 'comfort' boot

## Mary Janes

The Mary Jane was a popular evening shoe. It had a single strap across the vamp fastened by a button. It was often embellished with beading and embroidery.

## Colonial Style

The 'colonial' was another evening shoe with a large tongue and buckle, similar to 18th century French styles.

A Louis
heel tapers
in here

## Louis Heel

The hourglass-shaped 'Louis' heel was the height of fashion. It found its way onto everything from riding boots to formal leather boots and dainty evening shoes.

# The 1920s

In the Jazz Age of the roaring 1920s, women shortened their hair and their hemlines and with the shoe more visible, designers began to have more fun.

Josephine Baker was a Parisian actress and dancer who popularised the 'Charleston' dance. Her playful performances and fashion embodied the joyfulness of the decade.

## Oxford Shoes

Men wore Oxford shoes rather than boots. Oxfords have shoelace eyelets under the vamp in what's called a 'closed lacing' system. Made of leather or canvas, they evolved into a range of styles and continue to be the most popular men's shoe today.

## T-Bar Shoes

T-Bar shoes with a small heel were perfect for dancing. They were often embellished with satin, embroidery, rhinestones and buckles.

## EGYPTO-MANIA!

The discovery of Pharaoh Tutankhamun's tomb in 1922 set the world spinning in an Ancient Egypt-inspired craze for geometric patterns, metallic finishes and bright fabrics. Heels were often decorated with crystals and Art Deco patterns.

SPOTLIGHT ON

# André Perugia

The revolutionary shoe designer André Perugia trained in his father's shoe workshop and opened his first store in 1909, when he was just 16. During the First World War, he worked in a factory that made aircraft components. This taught him to appreciate the importance of engineering and precision in all forms of design.

"A pair of shoes must be perfect as an equation and refined down to the last millimetre, like a piece of an engine".


## The Mask Shoe

The Mask Shoe was inspired by Commedia dell'Arte - Italian masquerade theatre from the 17th century.

Perugia combined his meticulous approach with a child-like playfulness. He is known to have had long conversations with his shoes as he made them. They have so much personality, you can see why! His eccentric designs feel as fresh today as they did in the 1920s.

## The Fish Shoe

The Fish Shoe was inspired by the work of Cubist artist Georges Braque. It is made of suede with individual, layered scales.

## Monkey Fur Boots

This shoe was made for the surrealist fashion designer, Elsa Schiaparelli, who was inspired by new theories about the subconscious mind. The top of the boot is covered in long, silky hair so the wearer looks like they have animal feet.

# The 1930s

The 1930s were a time of economic depression and shoes were much less extravagant than they had been in the previous decade. Women's footwear was sensible, often with a chunky wooden heel. Cow leather was expensive, so shoes were often made of suede, which is made using cheaper sheep or goat leather. Colours were subdued with simple patent leather accents for embellishment.

## Court Shoes

The court shoe (pump) was a new innovation. This slip-on shoe was comfortable and versatile, and lasted as a trend throughout the decades that followed. Some court shoes had a slingback to save on leather.

# The Golden Age of Hollywood

Lana Turner

Going to the cinema became a popular form of escapism in this troubled decade. The fashions of Hollywood movie stars filled the pages of magazines and quickly set new trends for those who could afford them.

Bally Sandal, 1939

Strappy, heeled sandals worn by actresses like Ginger Rogers and Lana Turner showed more flesh than ever before. White was the most popular colour, but pastel or even metallic leather was worn for evening wear.

## Wingtip Brogues

Low-heeled, wingtip brogues became popular. They had a leather overlay that made a 'W' shape on the toe. They often came in contrasting colours.

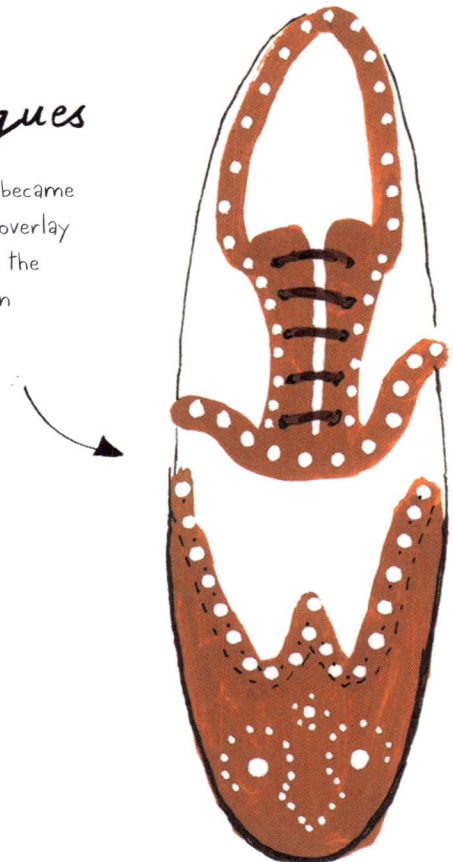

SPOTLIGHT ON

# Salvatore Ferragamo

Salvatore Ferragamo was born in Italy in 1898, and started learning the craft of shoemaking when he was just 11 years old. At the age of 18, he moved to the United States and eventually found his way to Hollywood, designing footwear for the silver screen – first rugged cowboy boots, then elegant sandals and sky-high heels.

His blend of avant-garde style and everyday comfort quickly made Ferragamo the go-to 'shoemaker to the stars,' supplying icons like Audrey Hepburn, Joan Crawford and Marilyn Monroe.

## Rainbow Wedges

These lightweight cork wedges were designed for Judy Garland. They were modelled to the foot, so despite their 12 cm height, they were comfortable to walk in.

In 1927, Ferragamo returned to Italy to open a workshop that handcrafted hundreds of designs for export back to America. When the 1930s brought a leather shortage, Ferragamo turned necessity into opportunity. Experiments with wood, wire, felt and raffia produced fresh looks that brought much-neeeded glamour and optimism to the uncertain times.

## Invisible Sandal

Designed in 1948, these shoes were one of the earliest examples of the use of plastic in footwear. The dramatic heel was inspired by the stern of the ship that carried Ferragamo back to Italy.

## Red Crystal Heels

Marilyn Monroe was known for wearing many pairs of Salvatore Ferragamo shoes, including these red stilettos covered in Swarovski crystals, which she wore in the film 'Gentlemen Prefer Blondes'.

# The 1940s

The 1940s were defined by the Second World War. Leather was mostly reserved for army boots, so shoemakers explored other materials like fabric, hemp, raffia and suede.

Low wedge soles became popular; there were peep-toe wedges and slingback wedges. In the summer, wedge espadrilles of raffia and cork were popular and for evening wear, a patent leather or suede platform heel.

Patchwork was a way of making use of suede off-cuts and preventing wastage. These Ferragamo patchwork wedges were sewn together with raffia.

Platform Heel

Peep-toe Wedge

Espadrille

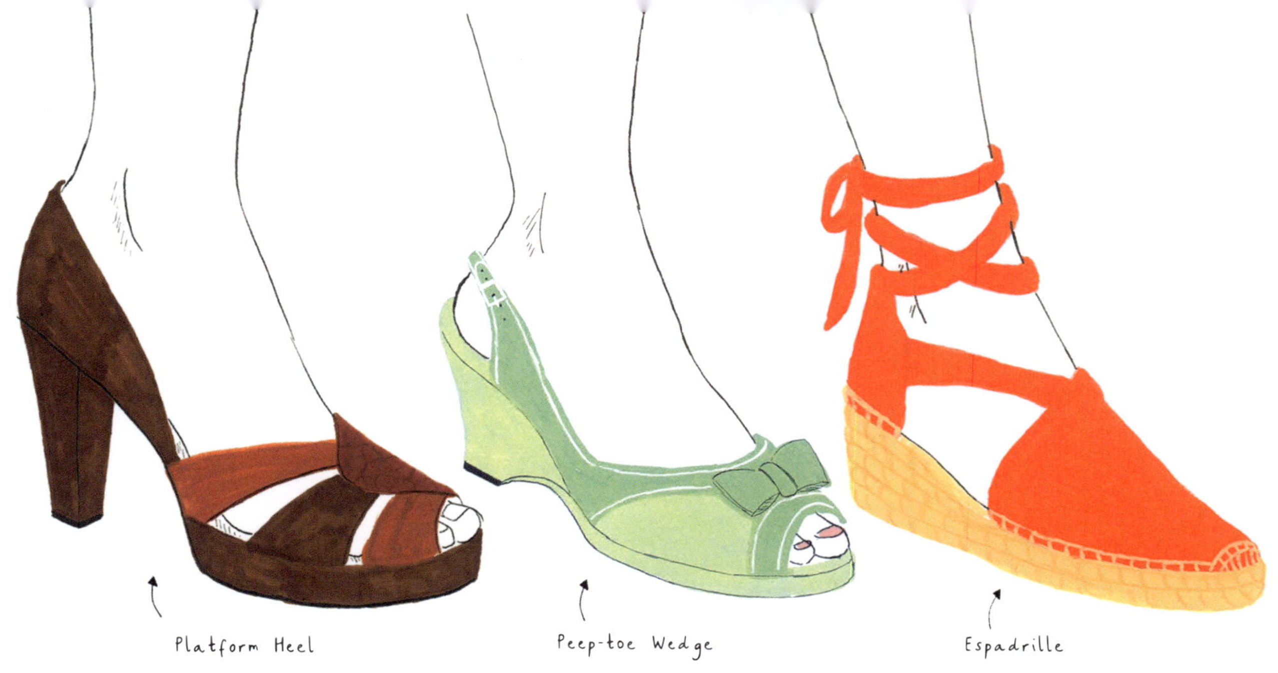

# Weejuns Loafers

In the United States, loafers gained popularity - they were simple, casual and smart. GH Bass made loafers with the name Weejuns. For embellishment, he added a diamond cut-out strap across the upper. In later decades, students would put a coin for a payphone inside the cut-out, earning them the name 'penny loafer'.

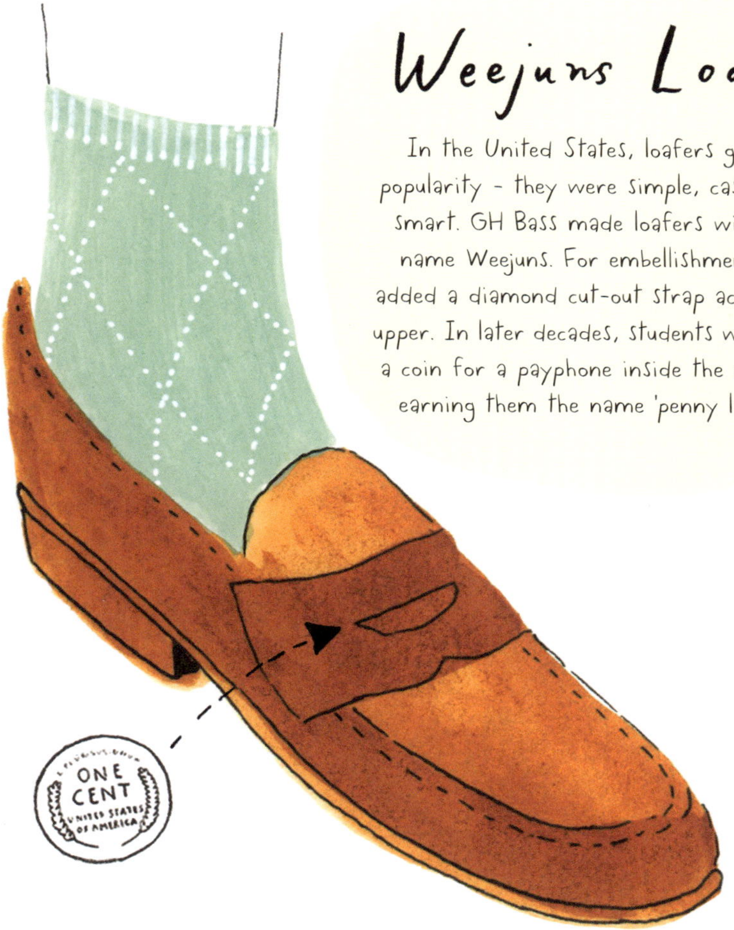

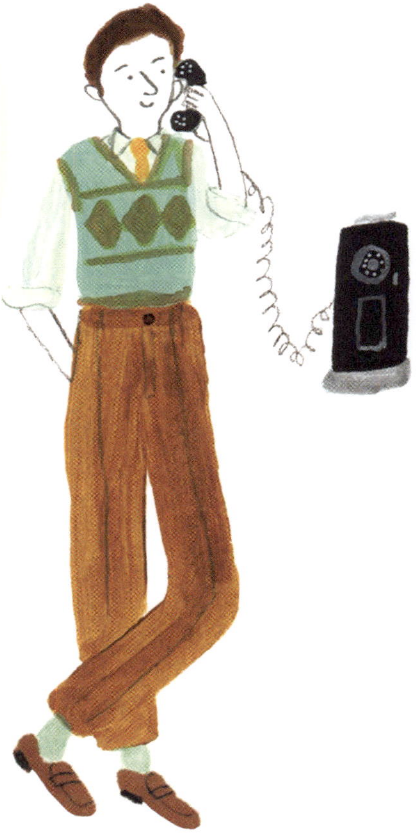

SPOTLIGHT ON

# Claire McCardell

Claire McCardell came from a wealthy, sporty Southern American family. In the 1920s, McCardell studied in Paris and taught herself to design by ripping apart samples by Vionnet and Chanel. When she returned to the USA, she utilised her skills to design comfortable yet feminine clothes for modern, sporty American women, featuring loose fits, hidden zippers, oversized pockets and fabrics that didn't require ironing.

During the war, street shoes were rationed but dance shoes were not. McCardell commissioned dancewear designer, Salvatore Capezio, to make ballet slippers with rubber soles in fabrics to match her garments.

I've always designed things I needed myself. It just turns out that other people needed them too.

Claire McCardell

The shoes were wildly popular and McCardell became the first female fashion designer to feature on the cover of 'Time' magazine.

SPOTLIGHT ON

# Desert Boots

The Desert Boot traces its roots to the South African military's lightweight 'veldskoene.' These ankle-high boots featured crepe rubber soles, low uppers, and just two or three eyelets, making them both comfortable for long marches and quick to slip on and off. Soldiers around the globe soon adopted the design for off-duty wear.

In 1941, British officer, Nathan Clark, stationed in Burma, spotted his men wearing veldskoene in their free time and decided to adapt the style for his family's shoemaking firm, C&J Clark.

The Clarks Desert Boot debuted at the 1949 Chicago Shoe Fair and soon became an international hit. Today, it still stands as a go-to smart-casual classic for men.

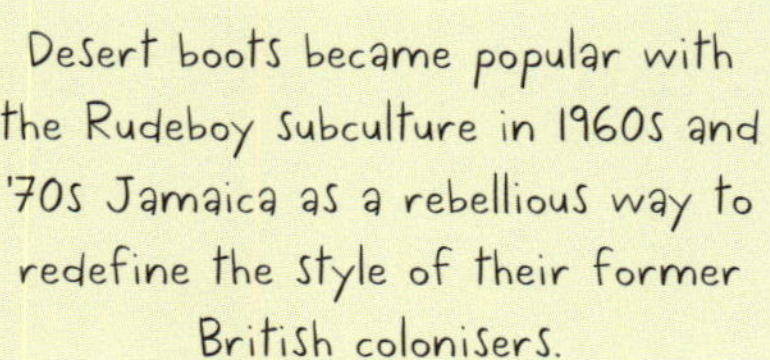

Desert boots became popular with the Rudeboy subculture in 1960s and '70s Jamaica as a rebellious way to redefine the style of their former British colonisers.

# The 1950s

After the war, spirits were high. People wanted to cast aside the plain, practical fashions of the '30s and '40s and embrace feminine chic and luxury fabrics. Dresses grew big, hairstyles grew taller... and so did heels.

The stiletto featured a moulded heel reinforced with a steel pin. Because metal is stronger than wood, less material was needed, allowing for slimmer, taller heels than ever before. They might not have been comfortable to walk in, but comfort was no longer essential!

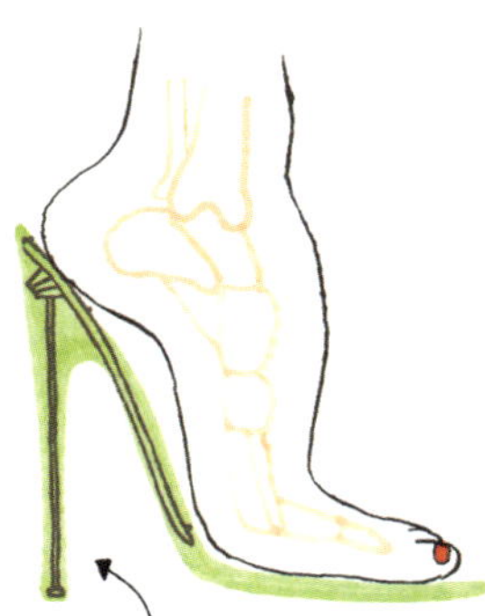

Steel Bar.

Stiletto Heel

## Kitten Heel

Worn by movie stars and singers, the stiletto became a powerful symbol of femininity and grace. By the end of the decade, kitten heels emerged as a more modest, easy-to-wear alternative to the stiletto.

Eartha Kitt

# Two-Tone Shoes

Two-tone shoes were popular with both men and women. The Spectator Shoe had one colour for the body of the shoe and a contrasting colour for the toe and heel cap. For teenagers and young girls, saddle shoes were a type of Oxford shoe in contrasting colours of black and white.

SPOTLIGHT ON

# Roger Vivier

French designer Roger Vivier first trained as a sculptor and his shoes have an undeniable sculptural elegance to them. He was one of the pioneers of the stiletto, embellishing his architectural heels with pearls, beadwork and lace. From 1953 to 1963, Vivier worked with the groundbreaking French fashion designer, Christian Dior, making couture shoes to complement Dior's elaborate, feminine gowns.

## Aiguille Stiletto

Released in 1954, this shoe made the models' legs look much longer, lifting the bum and accentuating the curves of the body. It was an instant hit.

## Belle Vivier

A black pump with a large chrome-plated buckle that became a fashion statement in the 1960s. Catherine Deneuve wore the shoes in the 1967 film 'Belle de Jour'.

## Coronation Shoes

Gold kid-leather sandals encrusted with rubies, designed for the coronation of Queen Elizabeth II in 1953.

SPOTLIGHT ON

# Coco Chanel

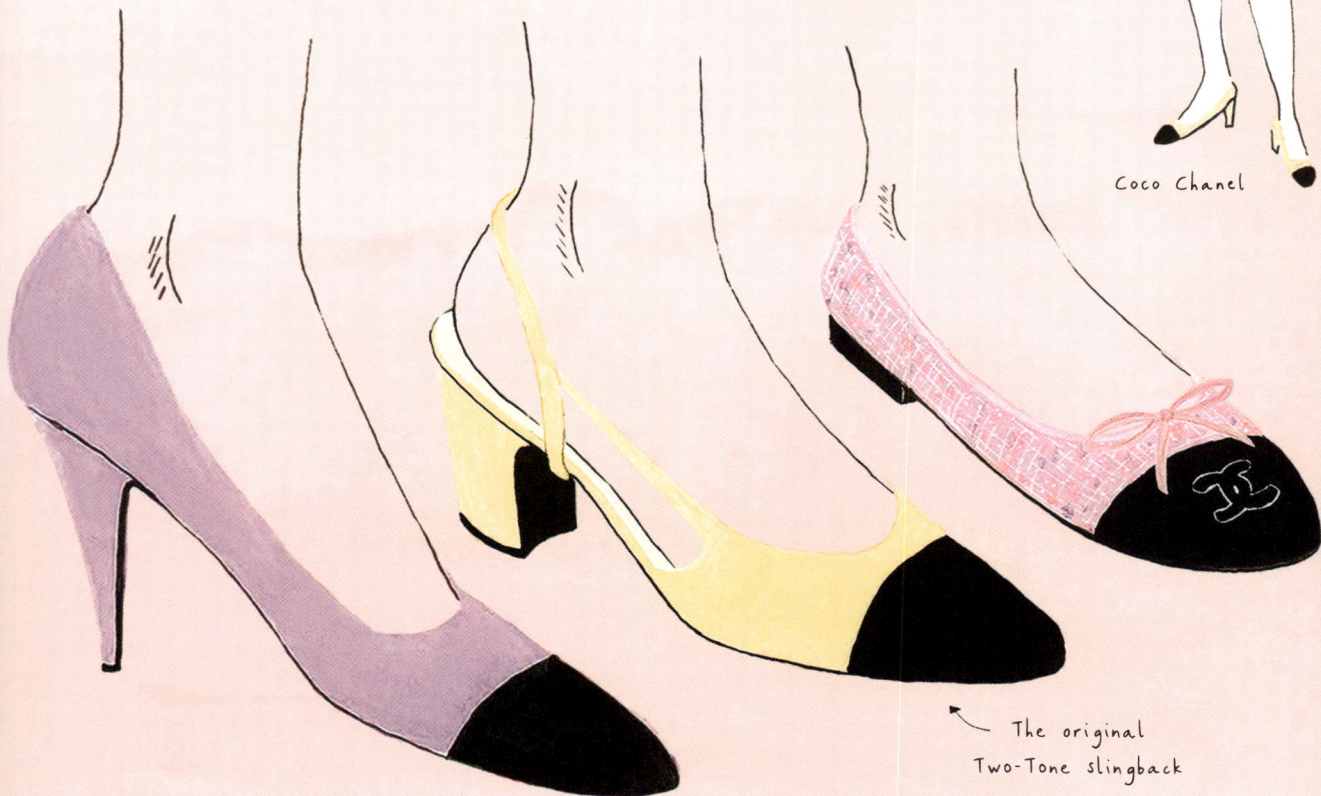

Coco Chanel was known for designing timeless, comfortable and elegant clothes for modern women. In her own words: "I don't do fashion. I am fashion." In 1957, she designed a slingback shoe inspired by men's two-tone shoes. The beige colour made the wearer's legs look longer, whilst the black toe made the foot look smaller. The low, chunky heel was both comfortable and stable.

The shoe was an instant hit and became a signature of the Chanel brand. It was embraced by celebrities like Brigitte Bardot and Jackie Kennedy.

Over the years, the two-tone shoe was reimagined in various colours and materials; tweed and satin, with a little bow and without, a squared off heel and a tapered heel, and an open and closed back. In all its versions, it stood out for its versatility - equally at home with a pair of casual trousers or an evening dress.

Coco Chanel

The original Two-Tone slingback

# The 1960s

Far Out!

Like the 1920s, the 1960s was a decade for the young. Kids who had been born after the war wanted to leave the hardship behind and have fun! The elegant, ultra-feminine looks of the 1950s were out and cheap, comfortable, playful clothes were in. Factories mass produced clothes and shoes in new materials like plastic and vinyl.

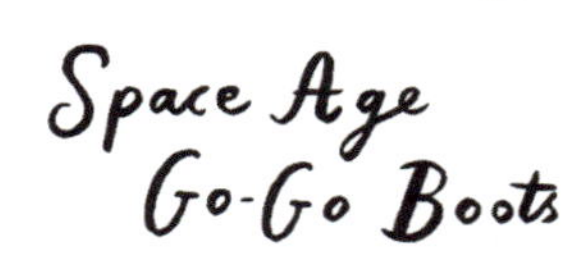

## Space Age Go-Go Boots

Daring miniskirts and hot pants were all the rage. They were worn with tall, tight boots, often in futuristic colours and patterns. White and silver were particularly popular, capturing the space craze inspired by the race to the moon.

Patent leather boots by André Courrèges

Vinyl boot by Pierre Cardin

## Mary Janes

Shoes were girlish with Mary Jane straps, rounded toes and low, square heels. Traditionally made of black patent leather, they now came in bright, poppy colours.

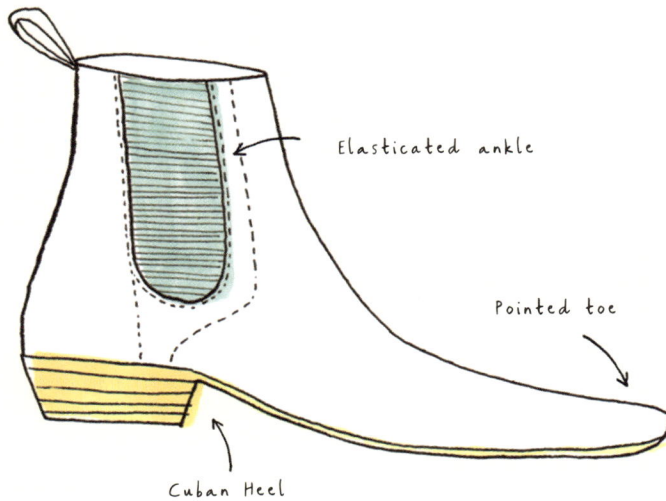

Elasticated ankle

Pointed toe

Cuban Heel

## The Chelsea Boot

The Mods (short for Modernists) were a youth subculture in 1950s and 1960s London, who were known for their cool fashion, music and motor scooters. Chelsea boots, which had elasticated sides instead of laces, complemented the sleek mod silhouette, fitting under the slim trousers of their sharp tailored suits.

SPOTLIGHT ON

# Mary Quant

Mary Quant captured the look of freewheeling, experimental, swinging '60s London. She is most famous for her miniskirts and short jersey dresses, but Quant believed that a 'look' went from head to toe, and she designed everything from tops to tights, hats and even makeup. In the early '60s, she launched her Quant Afoot range. It paired cheap but durable materials, like plastic, with bright colours and simple lines.

These half-boots were made from clear plastic over a coloured jersey lining. The soles were embossed with Quant's distinctive daisy logo so that the wearer would leave a trail of branded footprints wherever she went.

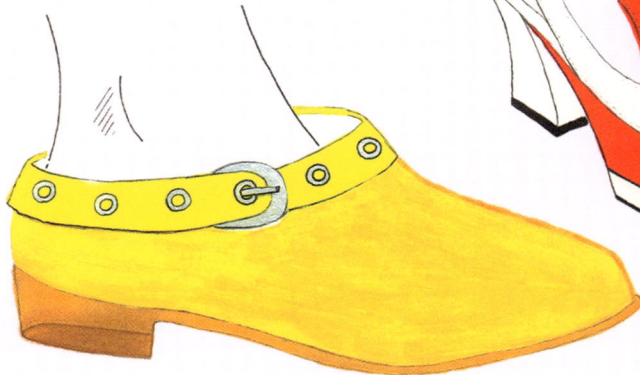

Later on, in the '70s, Mary Quant designed brightly coloured platforms and clogs to match the proportions of flared trousers and maxiskirts.

SPOTLIGHT ON

# Beth Levine

On the other side of the Atlantic, New York designer Beth Levine was also channelling the playful energy of the era.

Levine is most famous for popularising the boot in women's fashion. Made of new materials like vinyl and spandex, they were in such high demand that the department store, Saks Fifth Avenue, opened a special section in its shoe department called 'Beth's Bootery'.

These mules were daringly minimal. They had no sides and no back. A hidden elastic strap called a 'Spring-o-lator' secured the foot to the shoe.
The Stocking Boot was an experimental design made of a pair of stockings with a heel inside the fabric.
One of these days these boots are gonna walk all over you!
Nancy Sinatra made Beth Levine even more popular when she wore these go-go boots for her 1966 hit, 'These Boots are Made for Walkin'.

# The 1970s

The daring go-go boots of the '60s became mainstream in the '70s. They were tight fitting with a zip, reaching just below the knee, usually in earthy tones. They were paired with maxidresses with slits in them to show the leg.

Clogs became popular with the flower power hippies of the '70s. They were inspired by traditional shoes of Scandinavia and usually had a wooden sole and a block colour or patterned leather upper.

Musical diva, Diana Ross, was a fashion icon of the '70s.

Clogs

# Platforms

In the 1970s, disco music was where the party was at and platform boots were the shoes to wear on the dancefloor! They had a thick sole and a high heel and came in wild glitter and bright patterns. One pair even had a goldfish swimming in the heel! Glam rock bands, punk rockers and stars like Elton John and Freddie Mercury all had their own spin on the platform shoe.

Disco Go-Go Boot
Custom-made for Elton John.
Knee-highs worn by Gene Simmons of KISS.
Let's BOOGIE!

SPOTLIGHT ON

# Terry de Havilland

Terry de Havilland came from a family of British shoemakers and was known as the 'rock 'n' roll cobbler'. He used metallic leathers, reptile skin and shiny plastic to create brash, eye-catching shoes of all descriptions; cowboy boots, wedges, platforms and stilettos. His customers included rockstars such as David Bowie, Cher and Marc Bolan.

David Bowie wore these two-tone platform brogues in the music video of 'Life on Mars'.

## Snakeskin Brogue

A platform shoe in a patchwork of iridescent, textured leathers.

## Margaux Wedge

A brightly patterned, high wedge shoe that remains popular today. De Havilland once said: "My shoes have always appealed to flaunters. They're not for the faint-hearted."

## Rocky Horror

These custom platforms were worn in the camp, cult-classic movie, 'The Rocky Horror Picture Show'.

SPOTLIGHT ON

# Birkenstock

Birkenstock was a German, family-run shoe business that dated back to 1774. The company's turning point came in 1896, when Konrad Birkenstock designed a contoured footbed, which was fitted to the foot's natural shape, providing orthopedic support.

The shoes proved popular with German soldiers returning from the war in the 1940s. However, Birkenstock's unfashionable image kept them niche until 1966, when German-American dressmaker Margot Fraser introduced them to Californian health food stores. Their simple, back-to-nature vibe caught on with West Coast hippies, launching Birkenstock into cult classic status.

## Arizona

The Arizona was designed in 1973 by Karl Birkenstock. A fan of brutalist modern architecture, Karl believed that the structure and construction of a shoe should be a visible part of its design.

The Arizona is an open slide sandal with a cork footbed and two adjustable straps. It is still the bestselling Birkenstock sandal today.

# The 1980s

In the 1980s, mass production became cheaper and more efficient. Factories moved from Europe and the USA to Asia, making fashion even faster and more affordable. New looks came and went with the seasons.

The '80s were a time of wealth. Young professionals, known as yuppies, were keen to flash their cash on expensive brand name designers. Women rose in the corporate world, dressing to impress with sharp skirt suits and big shoulder pads. They paired this look with pointy toed kitten-heeled shoes.

Joan Collins starred in the hit TV show, 'Dynasty'. Her glamorous costumes and killer heels were the definition of '80s power dressing.

# Jelly Shoes

Jelly shoes made of moulded plastic were a hot trend. They originated in Australia in the '60s but took off in the USA in the '80s. They came in a range of shapes and colours, often with glitter embedded in the plastic.

# Madonna

Madonna was an '80s style icon. She paired bra-tops, ripped jeans and big studded belts with high, strappy, black stiletto sandals.

SPOTLIGHT ON

# Dr Martens

Not everyone was impressed by the flashiness of the decade. British youth subcultures like punks, skinheads, goths and indie kids set themselves apart from mainstream culture by wearing clunky Dr Martens workboots, which they styled with anything from black skinny jeans to miniskirts or ditsy floral dresses.

Joe Strummer of The Clash

Dr Klaus Maertens designed the boot in 1945. Recovering from a war injury, he fashioned an air-cushioned sole to make walking more comfortable. A British company bought the rights to his designs in 1960 and added the distinctive yellow stitching. They released an eight-eyelet cherry-red leather boot to the UK market on 1st April 1960 (1/4/60). The 1460 was the most popular boot throughout the '80s and it remains so today.

Air Pockets

Goodyear Welt

Moulded Sole

SPOTLIGHT ON

# Cowboy Boots

Cowboy boots originated in Spain and spread to the Americas in the early 16th century. They were designed for horse riding. A loose upper meant that the rider could slip their leg out if they were knocked off the horse; the slim toe allowed the foot to slide into the stirrup and the angled heel prevented the foot from slipping out.

They were glamorised in 1930s Hollywood Westerns as symbols of rugged independence and American ideals. In the 1980s, the New York party scene embraced the rebellious, carefree spirit of cowboy boots, pairing them with everything from miniskirts to skinny jeans.

Lucchese Cowboy Boots, designed for the cheerleaders of the Dallas Cowboys, 1989.

# The 1990s

'90s fashion was much more minimalist and lower maintenance than fashion in the '80s. Looks were stripped back and deconstructed. Anti-fashion became a trend in its own right.

## Prada 'Ugly' Shoe

This shoe was declared the 'ugliest shoe in fashion' by Vogue in 1996.

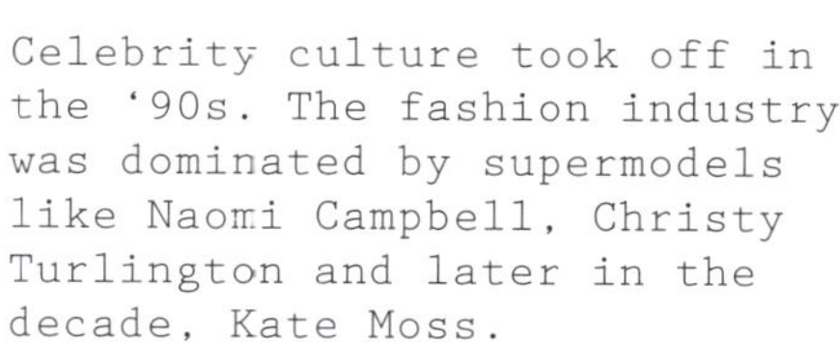

Celebrity culture took off in the '90s. The fashion industry was dominated by supermodels like Naomi Campbell, Christy Turlington and later in the decade, Kate Moss.

Miuccia Prada designed a pair of 'Ugly Shoes' with a chunky, clunky heel. She stated, "If you can wear these weird shoes, it means you're special... you have to be brave."

Miuccia Prada

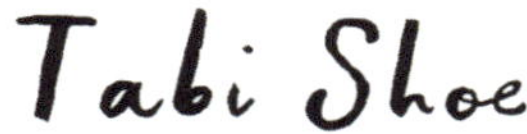

## Tabi Shoe

Designer Martin Margiela also embraced the bizarre with his Tabi Boot, which had a cleft toe, making it seem animal-like.

# Buffalo Platforms

Casual fashion was popularised by grunge bands like Nirvana. Other pop groups put their own sporty spin on casual-wear.

Platform shoes, which had gone out of style in the '80s, came back in with a sportswear edge. German company Buffalo created a platform trainer that was eye-catching and comfortable to dance in.

Emma Bunton, also known as Baby Spice.

Buffalos were introduced to mainstream culture by popstars the Spice Girls. These leopard print Buffalos were worn by Scary Spice in 1997.

SPOTLIGHT ON

# Vivienne Westwood

Together with her then partner, Malcolm McLaren, Vivienne Westwood was the founder of the punk movement in 1970s London. Although the money-drenched '90s felt a long way from the anti-establishment rage of punk, Westwood continued to design provocative, subversive looks that mixed historical influences, British identity and the rebellious spirit of punk.

## Pirate Boots

Inspired by portrait paintings from the 17th century, these shoes gave the romance of the highwayman a modern twist with three tongues and a low platform.

## Elevated Ghillie Platform

These towering 30 cm platform heels were influenced by the romantic ribboned shoes of the 18th and 19th centuries. They were made famous when supermodel Naomi Campbell tripped on the catwalk of Westwood's 1993 Anglomania collection, landing squarely on her bum.

SPOTLIGHT ON

# Manolo Blahnik

Manolo Blahnik was a self-trained shoe designer who came from the Canary Islands. He found fame in 1980s New York with his feminine, sculptural heels. The hit 1990s show 'Sex and the City' made Blahnik a household name.

I'm not afraid of heights, have you seen my shoes?!

Carrie Bradshaw of 'Sex and the City'

## The Sedaraby d'Orsay

A minimal, classic shoe with open sides made famous in 'Sex and the City' when Carrie's pair goes missing, so she decides to marry herself in order to get them back as a wedding gift.

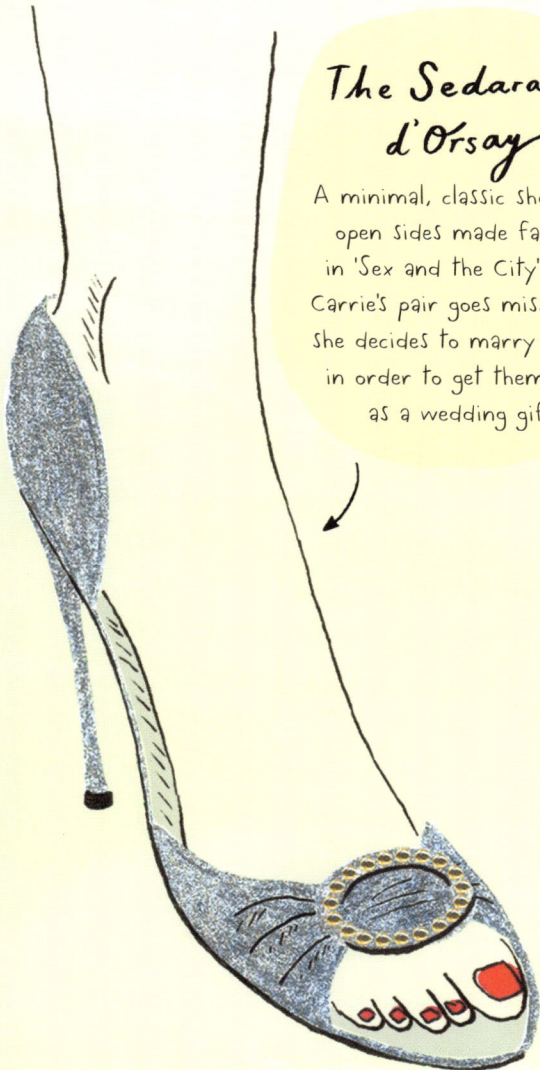

## The Campari

This shoe, designed in 1994, was inspired by a photo of the model Kate Moss. The girly, youthful Mary-Jane style is made ultra-feminine by adding a stiletto heel, a pointed toe and a grosgrain trim.

# The 2000s

The fashion of the 2000s, now known as y2k fashion, was glitzy, tacky and fabulous. Lacy camisoles were paired with low slung camo cargos, and tiny denim shorts were worn with big-buckled belts and a slogan baby-t. The shoes of the era were equally outlandish with oversized, cartoony silhouettes.

Super-long, pointy pumps were designed to poke out of the low-waisted bootcut jeans that were so popular.

Clear plastic slides were a trend.

## Gladiator Sandals

High-heeled gladiator sandals had thick straps that looked like cages, with a spine up the back of the leg. Some had a fringe at the top.

Founded in 1969, Moon Boot was inspired by the shape of the anti-gravity boots worn by astronauts. They became popular ski boots, but went out of fashion in the '80s. They made a comeback in the 2000s, when they were paired with miniskirts or hot pants.

## Uggs

Uggs ruled supreme. Australian surfer Brian Smith introduced the sheepskin boot to California in the '80s, but it wasn't until 2000 that the Ugg really took off, featuring on Oprah and swiftly on the feet of celebrities worldwide.

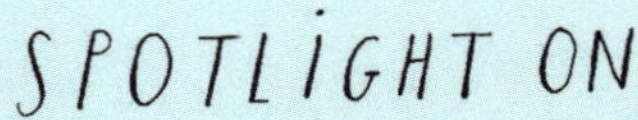

# Tory Burch

The Reva flat was a ballet shoe inspired by designer Tory Burch's mother, Reva, who used to wear a similar style in the 1960s. It first made an appearance in 2006. Coming in a range of colours, it had a leather upper, a rubber sole, a comfortable elastic heel, and the designer's giant double-T logo at the front. Priced high but not impossibly high, it became a popular, affordable luxury brand.

A matching Tory Burch baguette bag completed the look.

Reva Ballet Flat

SPOTLIGHT ON

# Crocs

Colorado natives, Lyndon 'Duke' Hanson and George Boedecker Jr, founded Crocs in 2001 as a boating shoe inspired by the shape of traditional Dutch clogs. Made of a lightweight foam resin, the waterproof shoe had a grippy sole and was easy to slip on and off. It was named after the amphibious crocodile, as it was designed to perform on both land and sea. Its ugly-cute quirkiness and practicality quickly caught on, not just as a boating shoe but for everyday wear.

Chapter 3

# BURNING RUBBER:

## The History of Sneakers

# INVENTION of the SNEAKER

Trainers, sneakers, runners, tennis shoes - whatever you call them, they're comfortable, stylish and they are everywhere you look.

The history of sneakers starts in 1839, when inventor Charles Goodyear began treating rubber with sulphur, making a tough, durable material called vulcanised rubber. Waterproof, hard-wearing and lightweight, this was the perfect material for the soles of shoes.

In 1876, the New Liverpool Rubber Company designed shoes with rubber soles and canvas uppers, which they called 'plimsolls'. They quickly caught on as a sports shoe for wealthy Victorians to wear on their tennis and croquet courts.

## Plimsoll

The plimsoll line of a ship is where its hull meets the water's surface, which looks like the line separating the canvas upper and the rubber sole.

## The El Dorado

A rubber high-heeled woman's tennis shoe from the 1890s.

Soon, the US followed suit. In 1892, the US Rubber Company began selling modified plimsolls with thicker soles and laces. In 1916, these shoes were rebranded under the name Keds. This was the first mass produced sports shoe and it became especially popular with women.

In America, the shoes were called sneakers because their rubber soles meant you could quietly sneak up on people!

## Keds Champion

The Keds Champion was designed for women in 1916, in a style that reflected the popularity of lace-up boots. They were advertised as follows: "Equally at home on the dance floor, the beach... the tennis court, the golf course - anywhere the fashionable fold congregate."

# EARLY BALLERS:

## The Story of Converse

The Converse Rubber Shoe Company was established in 1908 by Marquis Mills Converse from Massachusetts, USA. It started off selling rubber boots and car tyres.

Basketball was an exciting new sport in the USA, and in 1916, they introduced a new line of high-top shoes for basketball players, branded as 'Non-Skids'.

In 1922, basketball player Charles 'Chuck' Taylor walked into the Converse office and complained of sore feet. The company took on his suggestions for changes, making the shoe more flexible and supportive. Then they hired him as a brand ambassador. Chuck Taylor All Stars were born.

The Original Converse All Stars, 1922

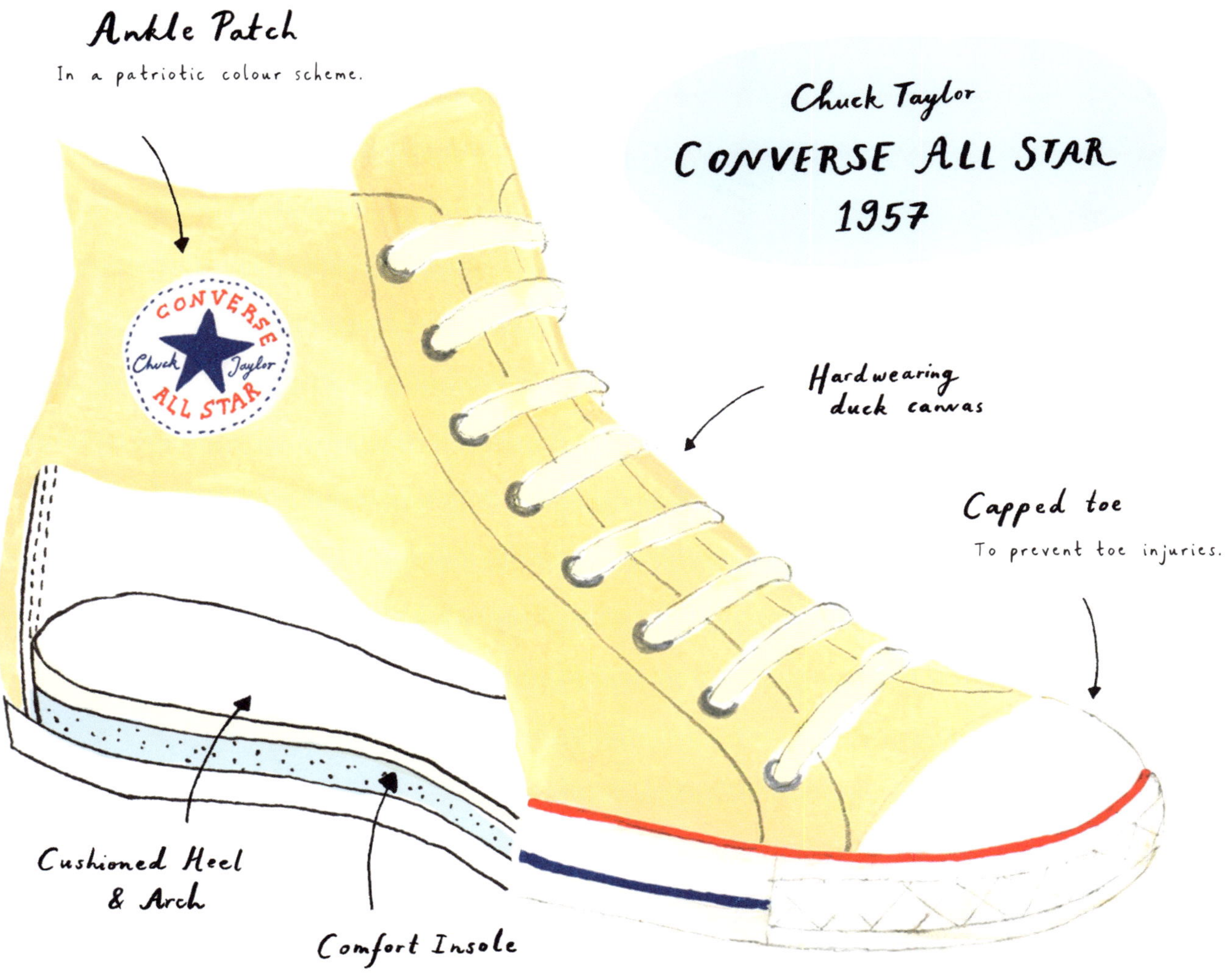

Chuck Taylor

# CONVERSE ALL STAR 1957

**Ankle Patch**

In a patriotic colour scheme.

CONVERSE Chuck Taylor ALL STAR

**Hardwearing duck canvas**

**Capped toe**

To prevent toe injuries.

**Cushioned Heel & Arch**

**Comfort Insole**

By the 1950s, Converse were not just the shoe of choice for athletes but also for an emerging youth culture. Young people were drawn to the informal, rebellious look of sneakers and in 1957, Converse brought out a low-top All Star for streetwear.

Celebrities like James Dean and Elvis Presley were photographed in their All Stars, cementing their cool reputation.

For almost 50 years, Converse had almost a complete monopoly on the sneaker market. But it couldn't last. Sportswear brands across the world were eyeing up the American market and by the 1970s, Converse had to run fast to keep up...

James Dean

# ADIDAS & PUMA:

## The Tale of the Dassler Brothers

Rudolf and Adolf Dassler were brothers from Bavaria, in Germany. In 1919, they founded a sports company called Gebrüder Dassler Schuhfabrik, or Geda for short (Gebrüder translates as brothers).

Both the brothers were members of the Nazi Party and in 1943, Rudolf was drafted into the German army. In 1948, after the war, the two brothers had a massive fight and shut down the company. The reason behind the feud remains a mystery. It might be that their wives did not get on, or it might be that Rudolf suspected that Adolf had been responsible for his traumatic conscription into the German army.

Whatever the causes, each brother set up a new factory on opposite sides of the river in their hometown. Rudolf's company was called Ruda, which later changed its name to Puma, and Adolf's company was called Adidas. The rivalry fed into every aspect of life in the town - even marrying across company lines was banned!

In 1936, the legendary runner Jesse Owens won a gold medal wearing these Geda shoes.

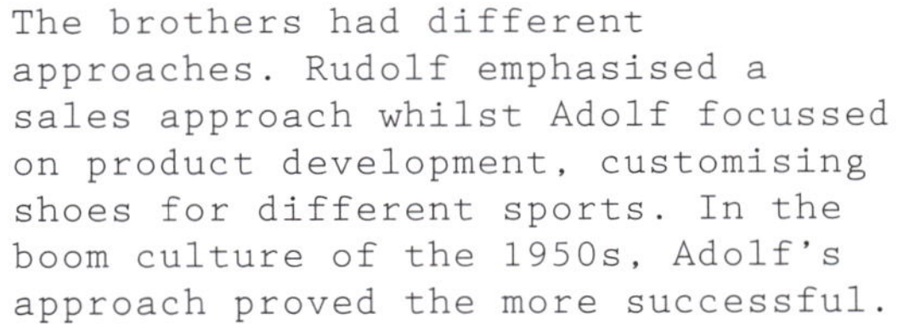

The brothers had different approaches. Rudolf emphasised a sales approach whilst Adolf focussed on product development, customising shoes for different sports. In the boom culture of the 1950s, Adolf's approach proved the more successful.

Both Adidas and Puma released football boots with screw-in studs, a development that had a big impact on the sport. Both companies still claim to be the first to develop the innovation.

Adidas Argentinas, 1954

Rudolf died in 1974 and Adolf died in 1978. They were buried at opposite ends of the local cemetery. Many business experts credit the rivalry and competition between Adidas and Puma for transforming sneakers into a multi-billion-dollar industry.

Puma Atom, 1950

# ICONIC ADIDAS SNEAKERS:

## SAMBA ORIGINAL

Designed in 1950 as a football boot for snowy, icy pitches, it featured an outsole with three cut-out suction cups, providing players with enhanced traction and stability.

## SAMBA ADV

A refined version of the Samba became popular with skateboarders in the 1990s. The ADV has a rubber outsole, reinforced stitching and additional padding.

## STAN SMITH

A classic, stripped back tennis shoe from 1965, which was first named after French tennis champ, Robert Haillet, but renamed after American champ, Stan Smith, in an attempt to capture the American market.

## COPA MUNDIAL

A football boot released in 1979 featuring an iconic black and white design and a fold-over tongue.

## SUPERSTAR

Designed in 1969, these sneakers became famous in 1986 when the band Run DMC released a song called 'My Adidas'. Adidas soon became a music subculture favourite.

## ADIDAS YEEZY

In 2015, Adidas released a collaboration with rapper Kanye West, who designed a bespoke version of the foam-soled Adidas Ultraboost. It sold out within ten minutes of release.

# The STORY of NIKE

Nike started out in 1964 as a company called Blue Ribbon Sports (BRS). It was a partnership between a young business graduate, Phil Knight, and his former track coach, Bill Bowerman. Bowerman was obsessed with his runners having the best shoes and was underwhelmed by the German sneakers that dominated the US market. BRS began importing shoes by a Japanese brand called Onitsuka Tiger.

Bowerman also experimented with his own shoe designs. In 1971, looking to make a shoe that would perform better on artificial track surfaces, Bowerman came up with the idea of pouring rubber into a waffle iron. The textured grid surface provided traction without using spikes and the waffle sole became a signature feature of the brand.

## Nike Cortez

Released for the 1972 Mexico Olympics, the Nike Cortez was the first shoe to use foam cushioning.

The success of BRS's innovations caused tension with Onitsuka Tiger and the two companies parted ways in 1972, with BRS rebranding itself under the new name Nike.

In 1976, Nike released an ad called 'There is no finish line' in which no Nike product was shown. The combination of audacious marketing and technical innovation was unbeatable. By 1980, Nike had gained 50% of the US athletic shoe market.

Phil

Bill

## Nike Swoosh Logo

The Nike swoosh was designed in 1971 by Carolyn Davidson, a Portland University student. Phil Knight famously said "Well, I don't love it, but maybe it will grow on me." She was paid $35 for her work.

# SLAM DUNK!

## NIKE AIR JORDANS

Nike's marketing strategy went from strength to strength, but the real turning point came when the company signed the basketball player, Michael Jordan, in 1984.

Jordan was a promising rookie for the Chicago Bulls. Despite his newcomer status, Nike offered him a huge payout to promote a new line of shoes, which they designed specifically for him in the colours of his team, black and red (known as the 'Bred' colourway).

The 'jumpman' silhouette logo didn't make it onto Air Jordans until 1988. The image was taken from an iconic photograph published in 'Life' magazine.

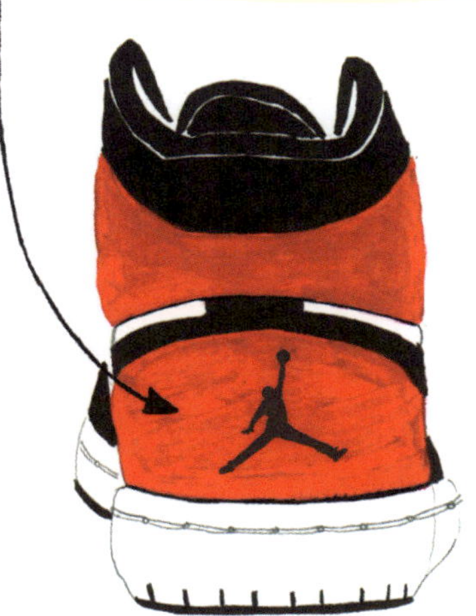

AIR JORDAN
BANNED!
"On September 15th, Nike created a revolutionary new basketball shoe. On October 18th, the NBA threw them out of the game. Fortunately, the NBA can't keep you from wearing them."
Air Jordan, From NIKE


The Air Jordan logo featured a winged basketball with 'Air Jordan' printed above.

NBA (National Basketball Association) guidelines stated that shoes must be 51% white. The fine for violating of this policy was $5,000 per game. Nike agreed to pay this fine and ran a TV ad called 'Banned' featuring Jordan in his Bred sneakers and the above voiceover.

The publicity from the controversy, combined with Jordan's skyrocketing success, resulted in the shoe earning $126 million in its first year, becoming the most successful single sneaker design to this day.

# 5 ICONIC NIKE DESIGNS:

## AIR PEGASUS

An affordable running shoe released in 1983.

## AIR FORCE ONE

This basketball shoe was designed by Bruce Kilgore in 1982. He took inspiration from a hiking boot with a lowered back, designed to reduce pressure on the Achilles tendon. He inserted air into the sole for shock absorption.

## AIR MAX 1

The first in the Air Max series, designed by Tinker Hatfield in 1987. It featured a visible air pocket in the heel.

## AIR MAX 95

From 1995, this sneaker had a gradient colourway in a ripple design and multiple air units.

## SHOX BB4

Released in 2000, the Shox used small rubber columns to absorb impact and return energy to the runner.

# Vans

California-based company, Vans, made simple deck shoes with thick soles. In 1974, legendary skateboarders Tony Alva and Stacy Peralta embraced the rugged look and grippy, flexible sole. Vans swiftly became the skater/BMX-er shoe of choice.

### Vans 98 'The Slip On'

An upgraded deck shoe, released in 1977.

### Vans 95 'The Era'

From 1976, this shoe featured a padded collar to protect the ankles of the wearer.

# New Balance

New Balance was founded in 1906 as a shoe specialising in arch support. It was a niche business until the '70s, when running became a popular leisure sport.

### NB 990

In 1982, these were the first sneakers to cost over $100. They were a status symbol that indicated that you were either serious about running or seriously wealthy!

# Reebok

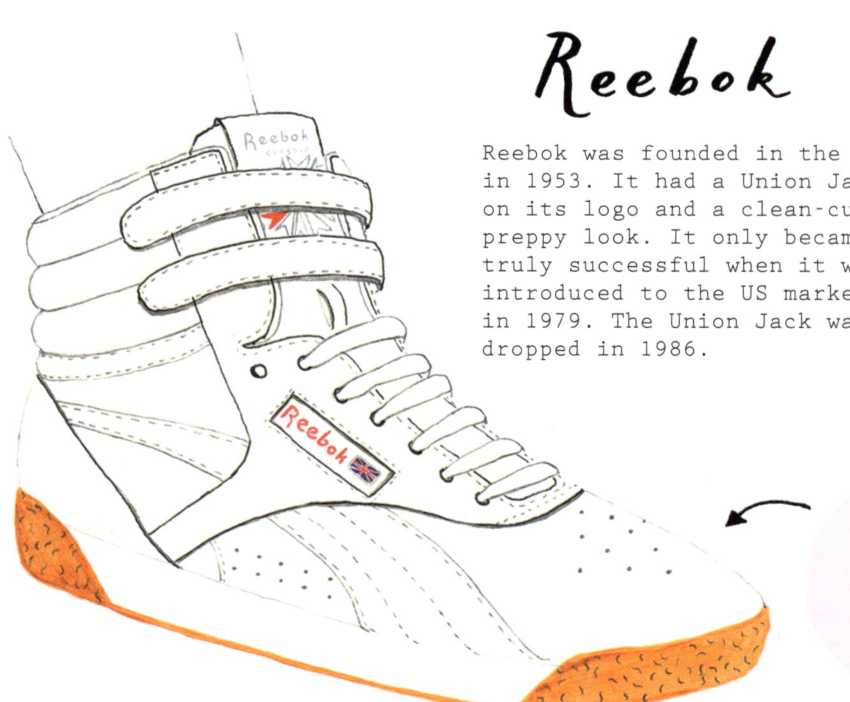

Reebok was founded in the UK in 1953. It had a Union Jack on its logo and a clean-cut, preppy look. It only became truly successful when it was introduced to the US market in 1979. The Union Jack was dropped in 1986.

Women don't sweat, they GLISTEN!
Jane Fonda

## Reebok Freestyle

Aimed at women, with a narrow, minimalist silhouette, the Freestyle became the shoe of choice for the aerobics craze in 1982.

## The Pump

Released in 1989, this basketball shoe had an internal inflation mechanism to provide a custom fit.

PUMP IT UP!

Basketball star Dee Brown won the NBA Dunk Contest in 1991 wearing Reebok Pumps. Before taking each shot, he theatrically pumped his shoes up. Reebok sales sky-rocketed.

# BEST FOOT FORWARD: The Future of Sneakers

Sneakers are the fastest growing fashion sector, with everyone from luxury brands to celebrities getting in on the action. Prada, Gucci and Louis Vuitton have all released their own sneaker lines, and Adidas, Puma and Nike have collaborated with athletes and artists such as Cardi B, Serena Williams and Kendrick Lamar to design limited runs that can sell for thousands of dollars.

## The Second-Hand Market

The second-hand market is also booming. Sneaker collectors will pay huge sums for vintage shoes and for valuable limited-edition collaborations. A pair of original Air Jordans were sold at auction in 2019 for 1.47 million dollars.

Nike Air Yeezy 2 'Solar Red' was a collaboration with Kanye West. The shoes were priced at $4,000 and up.

## New Technologies

Sneaker brands continue to innovate with new technologies to make shoes lighter, faster, cooler and more environmentally friendly. New materials like mushroom leather and sugarcane foam are paired with technologies like 3D printing to create ever more distinctive designs.

'Mylotm' by Adidas

'Nat 2' by Zvnder

Adidas and Zvnder are two brands experimenting with mushroom leather.

# FUTURISTIC SNEAKERS

## FAST-RB NITRO

Made by Puma with three carbon plates sandwiched inside 58 mm of high-tech foam and an elevated heel, this super-fast running shoe doesn't comply with World Athletics regulations, so can't be worn by professional runners.

## UNICORN SNEAKER

Made by Balmain out of calfskin and neoprene, these are statement sneakers!

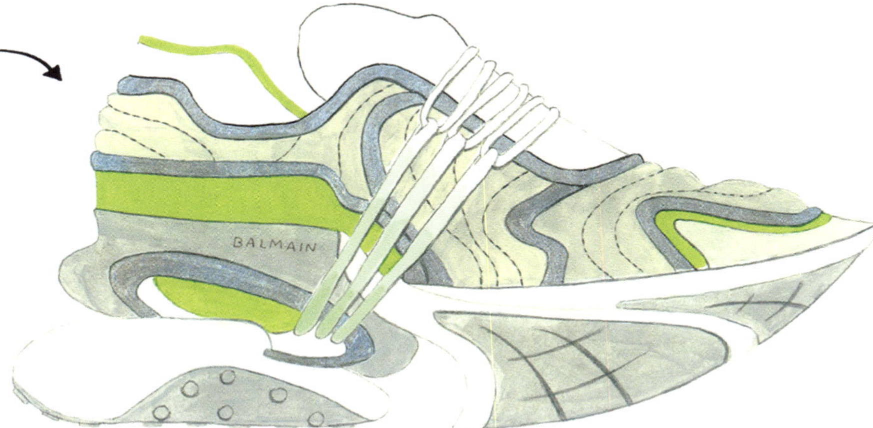

## CRAZY MAD IIINFINITY

Adidas's futuristic take on 1980s basketball shoes.

# So, what's next for shoe design?

The story of shoes is far from over. In fact, it's only getting more exciting. The future of footwear is set to combine sustainability, technology, and personalisation in bold new ways. Think smart shoes with built-in sensors and fitness tracking. Imagine materials made from plants or recycled plastics. 3D printing could soon let anyone customise or even create their own shoes, probably with the help of AI.

Old trends from the 20th century are making a comeback through the booming second-hand market, sparking new ideas for today's designers. Copies and lookalikes are everywhere, pushing big brands to get even more creative and personal with their designs. And while global brands may dominate the market, there will always be space for the daring, the different and the unexpected. Independent designers and creative risk-takers will keep redefining what shoes can be, just as they always have.

If you dream of becoming a shoe designer yourself, you'll need a strong interest in design, style, and how people move and live. You should enjoy drawing, thinking about trends and understanding what makes shoes comfortable and wearable.

Good shoe designers pay attention to materials, shapes, colours and how shoes are made. You'll also need to think about things like weather, sports and culture - different people need different shoes, and the best designs come from those who mix imagination with real-world problem-solving!

Whether you dream of designing your own line or simply want to express yourself through what you wear, one thing is clear: the world of shoes is wide open - you just need to step inside.

'Flames' 3D-printed shoes
by Zaha Hadid & United Nude

# INDEX

With love and thanks to Perry, Jo and Sam.

*SHOES!*

Text by Anna Davies
Illustrations by Daisy Wynter

British Library Cataloguing-in-Publication Data.

A CIP record for this book is available from the British Library
ISBN: 978-1-80066-057-1

First published in the UK in 2025, in the USA in 2026

Cicada Books Ltd
Studio 31a, Bickerton House
London, N19 5JT
United Kingdom
www.cicadabooks.co.uk



Printed in Poland on FSC certified paper